To Janie,

Jim and Betty Jo
are a wonderful Christian
that have really helped
me. I hope you
like my Book. God
Bless

Jim McFarland

A Spiritual Dance with Romance

A Spiritual Dance with Romance

Burns Harrison McFarland

INSPIRATIONAL
Publishing Co.

Inspirational
Publishing Co.

Published by R & A Inspirational Publishing Company
385 Highland Colony Parkway
Ridgland, MS 39157
www.inspirationalpublishing.com

Copyright ©2001 Burns H. McFarland
Cover and Interior Design by Mary Ann Casler
Production Manager: Tona Pearce Myers
Editor: Carlos Colón

First Printing, January 2001
ISBN 0-9706983-0-5
Printed in Canada on acid-free paper

10 9 8 7 6 5 4 3 2 1

It is early, yet early in the morn of my life;
So still and quiet, she whispers softly,
Yet not a sound she makes.

— Burns Harrison McFarland

Table of Contents

Dedication

This, my first book, is dedicated to my favorite friends and loved ones who have supported me through bad times, good times, and tough times alike.

My daughter and best friend, Anna Ryan McFarland, the most beautiful and brilliant daughter God could bless a father with, full of goodness, integrity, and patience. Besides being truly the greatest, similar to "Aunt Suzanne," she is very cool indeed, my counselor on life.

My best friend, Robert Burns McFarland, the most handsome, gentle giant and spiritual son God could bless a father with, commanding respect through love and courage. He is absolutely my inspiration.

My best friend, Robert Harrison McFarland, a truly Godly and dedicated Christian leader who has found his way into the history books in more than one chapter and, as my father, has been blessed with many opportunities to practice patience.

My best friend, Susan McFarland, and to many the most affectionate, understanding, beautiful mother God could bless a son with. To know and be around this lady is a treat beyond explanation.

To my best friend, Anna Hart McFarland Hazard, who exhibits beauty and grace as only a loving sister could. She is the greatest.

To my best friend and twin, Bobby Jo McFarland Gower,

who has always through generosity, understanding, forgiveness, and love, never left my side. She is my rock.

And to my best friend and special Guardian Angel, my hero growing up and today, Dr. Suzanne McFarland, my oldest sister. You don't find too many true geniuses with tons of common sense and the highest of reputation. She was known as a person who noticed one disabled or otherwise less fortunate being made fun of or having pity cast upon them. She would join them side by side and stake her life on their reputations. She was a gallant and valiant warrior and defender of the weak.

Time and money are important. Thank you for spending your valuable money to buy this book and thank you for spending your precious time to read it. Until this printing, the only pieces I had published were about business, mainly about legal- medical business, with one exception — the poem "Angelic Siblings," which appeared in a "Young Poets Cover" a few years ago in Virginia. That poem has now become the cornerstone of this book as well as the recent opening of "Angel on My Shoulder", an angel store in Jackson, Mississippi, and tons of inspiration our loving Heavenly Father has been kind enough to bless me with, and that has virtually changed my life again.

Publisher's Preface

A significant portion of this heart-filled romance collection is
The Song of Solomon, which is recognized as one of the
original romance poems from which all others originate. Chosen
as a primary feature to this book, the Song has inspired a num-
ber of poems that were written in similar style. These intermin-
gle with others of a more contemporary nature.

The poetry lends itself to a passion, refreshing in deep feel-
ings of romance and remembering those significant lovers of
times past. Several quotes and verses accent the message of love
from current as well as Biblical times.

As we embark on our initial journey into this arena of pub-
lishing, we must keep in the forefront two guiding principles.
The first is what the Chinese have long said, *"The journey of a
thousand miles begins with the first step."* The second principle
is: *"If ye have faith as a mustard seed, you shall say to this moun-
tain move from here to there, and it shall move; and nothing
shall be impossible to you."* (Matthew 17:20)

Robert Burns McFarland
Anna Ryan McFarland

A Spiritual Dance with Romance

Yesterday's Gift

Have you ever asked yourself if life could get any better? Have you told yourself if today is your last, will it surely be your best? These are fun questions to ask yourself, and it is a great way to feel. When these feelings come, we wish and often silently pray they will last forever and a day.

On the other hand, have you ever asked yourself if life could get any worse, and why is this happening to me? And have you further demanded, then begged that the unhappy, sad, lonely feeling end now? At such times have you considered if this nightmare continued in this direction, what would be the point?

Most of us, at best, have briefly experienced each range of extreme emotions, some more than others. I was in a meeting once, and the topic was attitude. . . . Is yours one of gratitude or complacency? My favorite response was given by a lady from New York's inner city who shared that hers was unquestionably both . . . depending on the day, events surrounding her, and maybe even the time of day. She futher shared that God is more willing to be found than she and I are willing to hunt for him, even though there is no place He cannot be found.

There have been moments in my life when I knew there was a God and that He was all powerful, all knowing, all loving to everybody . . . but me . . . and further the day would never come when He would show me the two things my children wanted and needed to know since before their first birthdays: (1) that they were loved for who they were; (2) that it was all going to be okay. I am thankful, to beat the band, that the above previous assumption turned out to be wrong, wrong, dead wrong!

As I gradually learned more of the majesty, forgiveness, and true compassion of The Living God, life became sweeter, more valuable, and much more fun to me.

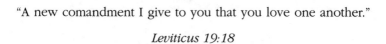

"A new comandment I give to you that you love one another."

Leviticus 19:18

"Great Thoughts always come from the Heart."

Marquis De Vanenargues

"All mankind loves a lover."

Ralph Waldo Emerson

LOVE

With tenderest of moments do I ever recall
Feeling the deep, yet sweet, of the last freefall.

From tomorrow's rising sun until no longer time will come.
Her face, the face, with warmth embrace,
Not until tomorrow, but yet until today.

Beauty abounds from sand to sea,
Ever fond my memory of thee.
For no matter days that pass or nights that go love remains.

Love, love, for what a fine sound
Doth ring and sing of this love.
Forever comes love, not ever from love,
That renders one spellbound.

Canst one live and yet not love?
I think not! For without love, what is life?
For whose love may tonight we speak?
Yours? Hers? His? I ask whose?
Silent, I whisper, if draw ye near.
Tonight, love is the love of true love, with no fear.

Angelic Siblings

*To My Three Sisters, Two Who Are Not Yet Angels
and One Who Already Is*

It is early, yet early in the morn of my life;
So still and quiet, she whispers softly,
Yet not a sound she makes.

To hear her closely, I must listen closely with my heart,
For not a sound she makes;
Her voice through memory speaks loudly in my mind
From yesteryear;
A year of youth, the end of which never seems to be.
Why?
Yes, tell me why we are so moved by sadness, gladness?
And the passion of happiness?

The light that shines within her heart
Continues to beat.
Ever so softly and ever so gently
Her spirit leads me.

Suzanne, Susan Ann, what a beautiful name has my angel.
No wonder she is a Guardian.
As Guardian, no wonder how busy she must be with me,
For time matters not to her.

For go I must, since time remains here for me,
As it is quiet again, yet not as early.
For I listen closely to hear her closely.
So still and quiet she whispers softly,
Yet not a sound she makes.

Take Away

Take away unnecessary sorrow and worry — today take away.
Take away hunger and hate we pray — take away.
Take away lows and blues from yesterday — take away.
Take away those whose trusts betray — take away.
Take away the frowning face display — take away.

Replace

Replace with a clear about-face — replace.
Drain to origins of our innocent birthplace — replace.
Standing firm with a true commonplace — replace.
For the smile becomes you so upon our face — replace.
Thus substituting the miracle of grace.

Take away and replace this day
A magnificent tomorrow
That shall arrive and stay.

The Heart

The heart must be my friend,
Yes, what a friend indeed, my heart
Bruised or broken,
In fact and in deed, it remains my friend.

As early as I can remember, its beating breath increases
As the look, touch, smell, a lovely one nears
The sparkle in her eye, the smooth tender skin
Her scent of honey
Could this not be God's most beautiful?
Or could it?

The heart cannot close! Can it?
What a sad tale would this be.
For life's happy times await the present
As closer and softer we move to open
Open? Open what? What else? — "The Heart."

Farther the shadow away as it flees,
From moment to moment, some Java, yes, please
Says Peter, my friend from round the border,
Border or borders, for tonight I now see
That my heart, my friend, life's key for me.

Endless Movement

It is with endless movement that I now think of thee.
For never and forever I wander and question to see.

Alone, alone through distant stars
Canst move further onward, but inward.
One thinks to feel toward the morning light
My vision from dream, yet clear from the night.

Continuously stepped I forward upon the vast open wild.
To touch God's hand in nature,
Done when I was child.

For when a soul is open to be as free
Leaned forward did she and tenderly kissed me.
For when test came, surely canst not she flee?
For with endless movement I now think of thee.

Foolish — Ghoulish

Foolish-ghoulish, today's theme I shall sing,
For if I sang
Would cause you to shoot
To-ma-to – To-mah-to at you know who.

Duck, I would, behind platform I shall,
Direct at Buddy I will,
For cousin could shift the drift away.

No fun's okay and okay's all right
As long as all your poems
Aren't too "uptight."

So tell, foolish-ghoulish, what's that all about?
Not so necessary we all know before we go,
I'd ask you, 'How would I know?"

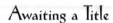

Awaiting a Title

Jiminy Crickets, Gee Whillikers, I'll be John Brown —
These are what I'll say, I didn't say yesterday,
If my face falls flat on the ground.

Tweedle Dee and Tweedle Dum
Fee fie fo fum
Who said that?
Beats me. Tom Thumb?

Well, well, so much for this and so much for that.
No matter what's up or what's going down
Lighten up, hip and hop, head on downtown.

What's this all about?
Not staying too heavy
If it's always too heavy
It can't be light or too uptight — well, good night!

Whisper

Softly and tenderly her name I whisper
To myself; but not out loud,
For stars and moons long since passed.
Time stood still, or so it seemed.

Days of laughter and nights of song
Are never forgotten,
But stored in mind and heart forever.
Forever, yet to return never,
For return thou canst and shalt not.

Yesterdays shall intact remain
For in remaining thou sight in vision;
To be seen through eyes of tears,
Tears of delight, twilight in creation.

Speak out loud I dare not;
Whisper softly, tenderly, I hear your name, my dear,
To myself I shall when no one is near.

Truth

Truth speaks through many a tongue, mind, and heart.
So whose truth do I speak when I speak to you?
Your truth as you speak to me?
I thank you for a part of you,
That part which is true.

Patience, kindness, forgiveness:
Who can deny this truth?

Yet, when a child is young, they know
More truth than many another —
Wouldn't you say?
As years pass, the truth tends to stretch, reverse, and confuse
That which was once simple.

So when tomorrow I wonder what was true yesterday,
I'll just find and ask a child,
"What is the real truth?"
And the littler the better.

A child, yes, a child — for the fan of a child am I.
A child I used to be — the only time this is not true
Is when a child I remain to be.

Dreams

Dreams are forever hidden in crevasses far, far away.
Away from outside disturbances.
Dreams, hidden forever, far away.

As daylight breaks and shadows flee, moments neatly tied.
As thoughts return of thee —
Tell if the memory was true, as is part of the experience
Hidden in dreams far away.

Cannot thee search for and return from where thou canst not hide?
Yes, the dream shall live on forever, long past my time —
Yes, indeed it must!

As eyes close and heart opens
A tender flight I shall never recall.
For a dawn nears farther and deeper than ever before.

Silence it nears to point of emotion.
Thou, canst not I speak, for what dreams unlock.

Tomorrow and tomorrow's tomorrow delight shall witness
Smile and laughter with happiness forever.
Hidden in crevasses of dreams.
Yes, hidden far, far away.

Spring

Come we again of this season to Spring
As anew it awakens from deep within
Birth begins its rebirth
As we come again to this season of Spring
For those who forever frown
They're forced to smile again,
Again, and again until habits they sing
Sing the song that's hidden within.

Step forward I choose to say
As if saying's doing, and doing's okay.
Move I shall, yet we'll soon see!
Moving, still moving, to be set free.

Come we again, this season of Spring,
For another dance with life,
Life so sweet, everlastingly kind,
Forgivingly spiritual until the end of time.

Today's Question

Whose question asked most of her?
Which reply did she really mean?
Could you tell me from what you saw?
Or did you see whose question asked most of her?

As she was asked where time had gone,
Did others notice the hidden frown?
Others whose time had left too soon,
Of which path and choice did they so choose to question?

If, in fact, I question now
Where indeed she had gone,
Would you go and show her how
To return now?
Now? For when is now?
As now is said it is no longer now,
But then.

Questions, questions, only questions —
I ask, canst some days
Be days of only questions?
As in questions today, or today's question?
Yes, ask now.

My Dearest Soul

Canst one speak of the soul,
As soul of "Heart and Soul"?
Do tell. How important can the importance stand, as one
Speaks of, dreams of, and envisions my dearest soul.
I'm glad, not sad, that my soul is in the hands of
The Father of Heaven.
As souls that are blessed, I feel mine to be
From origination day until eternity.

How then can one grip, snap, or let anger loose?
If such good shape is kept of soul,
From Father of above,
Do tell, How?

Not today, I shan't grip, snap, or let loose of anger,
But I shall thank, forgive, and forget...for the good of my soul.
Dare I will feel better and closer this way,
This day as I say to my dearest soul.

Was it Last Night?

As I awoke late, late last night,
Or was it last night?
All movement was ever so still
As if nothing, for even a moment, had in fact moved.

Monday's night, last night from tonight
Pen these words for tomorrow's night — now tonight.
Each place I go, each day I live,
Each face I see, a reminder of thee.
Come steal away, only for a moment, with me.

For more than one, too many I fear be
Hidden as stolen romance, then flee
As high as stars that hide in the sky
Only to return for you and for me.

Tears of laughter and sorrow so near
With heartbeat increasing, can you not hear?
Sense your footprints, so gently made,
As your tender touch upon my body is laid.

My eyes now close, traveling far, far away
Away from this time, yes, far away
To the night I speak of.
Tomorrow night? This night?
Or was it last night?

Recovery Friends

These are so, so very valuable friends, especially special friends
Friends in recovery
Recovery friends
Jimmy, Jenny, Jerry and Terri...Terry, Timmy, and Tammy
Mac, Jack, Ben, and Winn...Jeff and Criss...Carry and
Bob...and yes, Todd.
There's Joe and Jo...And Randolph...and of course Julie and
John.

I wonder what happened to Phil, or Jill, or James or Melissa?
Have you seen Bill, or Billy, or William? Where is Cathy or
Jackie or even
Jimmy? Try and find out where Janise and Dan and David
went.

I hope and pray again to see Teresa, Susan, and yes, Timothy,
and Lee...along with
Marcus and Sherry...and Tommy...and Tom.

You know it sure was sad to hear about Alvis and Allen, and
Jason and
Jessica...and Danny...I hope they come back someday...

You know there's got to be a special place in heaven for Ron,

And Donnie, and Roland, and Ricky . . . and James . . . and . . .
The rest of our special recovery friends.
God's miracle
One day at a time
The life of recovery
A special friend
A recovery friend

God, I know, has a lot of love to give
To care for our friends in recovery,
Yes, our recovery friends . . . especially two . . . me and you. . . .

Love or Lose

Canst one live and yet not love?
Question asked one — answer! Love or lose.
What doth love do? One may ask.
Make the world a better place.
To live, one may say.

Where comes love? One may question.
From the head, mind, memory, or soul?
From self, pride, prejudice, value of art?

Without love, what remains? Loneliness.
Unhappiness, anxiousness, sadness, and badness.
Life's future is hardly even barren —
Without love, what remains? Let us not discover.

Love is ultimate value, maximum indeed,
Ever flowing and growing to the point it should be
Without future and faith of mankind to perish
With all God's creation it shall forever cherish, forever flourish.

The Value of a Second Chance

As early I awoke this past Tuesday morn
Different it was than ever before.
I knew it, I just knew it.

My body, my mind, my heart did not feel the same.
My body, my mind, my heart did not seem the same.
My body, my mind, my heart were not the same.

Ask I did to my mother, my friend,
What has happened? What is wrong?
Ask I did to my father, my friend,
Where am I? Yet more, who am I?
No response; no answer; no key.

Who then knows where answers lie?
I lie awake, I cannot sleep; my condition worsens.

When long ago and memory dim, the key I do recall.
For on my knees in dark of night
To my Maker I would talk.
Life so sweet, so good to feel the love,
The spiritual warmth, the guidance of truly a Godly hand.

The memory now is brighter, clearer ever still.
There is to where I shall return even now.
My body, my mind, my heart is better, yes better,
Better even still, my body, my mind, my heart.

So better even still that now kneeling is a pain,

A pain I'll put off to another day.
A moment of more timing, convenience, less embarrassment.
Key? What key? My memory is fading fast
To a distant time.

God, what God? Did I hear you say God?
How soon I forget such educators, scholars, and lovers?
How soon? Too soon is how soon.

I try to sleep but cannot, when then I know not.
Yes, I see the morning brings
A reversal of fortune for me.

For as I awake, a gracious spiritual hand touches me.
Life will never be in reverse again for me,
For now I am truly set free.
I know, for I know it in my body, my mind, my heart.

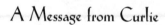

A Message from Curlie

(If you saw the movie <u>Cider House Rules</u>, you'll know Curlie was one of the most touching and sick, yet deserving, orphans. His sweet Heavenly Father decided to take him to the top of the mountain at a tender age. If you didn't see the movie, you should!) The movie and inspiration from Anna prompted the following:

Tonight I lie in my bed, by myself,
Wondering why I am so sad.
I don't have a Momma or a Daddy, and that's very bad.
Do you think God doesn't love me, or is life just not fair?
Tell me if you care.

All my friends have Mommas and Daddies.
Where do you figure they came from?
What do you figure I got to do to get one?
I hope tomorrow is not like today, 'cause I ain't got one.

When I close my eyes and dream of Heaven,
The first thing I see is Momma and Daddy
Holding my hand, rubbing my back, tucking me in,
Taking me to school, taking me to Church,
Just like all my friends, all my friends
That's got Mommas and Daddies.

When I get scared, I don't want the government lady
Or our neighbor, baby-sitter, or even my sister.
I want you to help me please, please help me.
Sometimes I want my "beo" and sometimes I want my "banke,"
But there is something I always want,
My Momma and Daddy...
Will you help me find them?

*I have learned so many lessons from Anna, one of which is
to seek those, especially children, who need God and His help. My
goal is to be half as willing and open to God's direction as is she.
(Before I sleep tonight as I try each night, I will kneel before my
Maker and thank Him for the grace and mercy He has shown me
for a long time, especially at this moment. As I think of Curlie
and other Curlies, I thank God for the gift of a Momma and
Daddy and loudly beg Him for the enthusiasm and willingness
to seek out and share with and help those who don't have or ever
will have a real Momma and/or Daddy. I ask you to please do the
same, now!)*

Letter to an Unknown Lover

As I pen this to you, I can't help
But think, wonder, pray, and question
Who in fact are you?
Days and months have passed since spoke we last.
No matter where I go or way I turn, there have you been.
Wonder I do, ask I shall, from first page to last, cover to cover
In my letter to an unknown lover.

The other lover, yet unknown, is not really known to me.
Let me paint her picture both to now see.
She may be tall, yet short, heavy yet light, dark yet white.
She may be loud yet quiet, handed from left or right,
Full of vigor not spite.

As she walks, she glides. I see her more with eyes shut than not.
As she was here she now is not.
Magically we speak, not yet to meet.
A cloud of rain, shining of sun, has now
Begun above us to hover.
Continuing to dream, write, feel to and yet from a letter
A letter to, a letter to an unknown lover.

Is it okay to ask a question, a question of much?
A question of GOD, a question as such?
When might you figure she might appear,
Stand beside me near?
Is that an okay question to ask of my love, my dear?
God, I know, knows and when I know,
I have little if any to fear.
I guess it's okay to write to her, about her, for her,
Wherever she may be.
To her I now write this letter, this letter to,
This letter to an unknown,
This letter to an unknown lover.

Tough Times

So you're disenchanted with life, disgruntled with them,
Upset with us
Since you have encountered, wrestled against,
And come to grips with
Tough times.

Yes, no fun the time, no prize the crime, no joke, no rhyme.
Tumbled through family help, money, and influence
Until all seemed lost.
So sad, so mad, they cried, still tried to make up for,
Cope with, explain away
The inevitable tough times.

Solution, a man said,
On knees one stood, before his Maker: asked, prayed, begged
to begin again?
A word seldom used, on knees she stood, and said, shouted,
screamed...softly yet soundly...
Please! Please! Help! Please understand!
Please lend a helping hand, please.

Suddenly it happened, yes, answered inside my heart
A light so bright, everlasting clear.
I had missed so much.
No more shall I look over my shoulder, or behind my back,
since I can now see
The value of, opportunities in, and miracles of tough times.

God's Special Moment

Today, this special day, unlike other days,
I think, dream, and live for
God's special moment.
Five steps forward, one step backward,
Or was it one step forward and five backward?
Ah, I remember now,
It was both, was it not?

Today as we move, live, breathe, touch,
Take from this creation, no day can be as special, as precious,
As tender as this day, today.
So one recalls miracles, sacrifices, forgiveness
That seemed to be from, come from, originate from
God's special moment.

Where do good things come from,
wonderful things spring from? Life start from?
Where, do you think, could one figure, have one question?
Where? Let us examine possibilities, probabilities.
Where I know, I think, I feel, I know
God's special moment.

So then let us say that this day we will see
What is open to view
As life is dictated by, who else, we including, who else, you.
This simple statement of life, I can barely understand,
Yet hardly repeat, for I am hopeful
And thankful of life's continuation
Of God's special moment.

"Thou shalt love thy neighbor as thyself."

John 13:34

"All, everything I understand, I understand only because I love."

Leo Tolstoy

"Love those that love you."

Voltaire

Cups Café

How about some Java, some company, some fun
At Cups Café?
How about it? Tuesday, Friday, Wednesday, what day
Shall we meet? A little safe, a little risqué
Not at Rick's, nor at Nick's, but Cups Café.

Let's drink from the fountain together, all together
The sweetest drink in town. They're all drinking,
singing, and swinging.
What else can we say? Who else can we see?
What time's the right time to swing, sing, and dance?
A cappuccino, an espresso, till tomorrow...Let's go to
Cups Café.

Spiritually Speaking

As days go by, questions arise, of the value
Relevance to, importance in, spiritually speaking.
As I listen, feel, and ponder God's will
I ask, pray, and consider what He may think of me?
Beginning the morning on my knees, I beg my maker
Ending the evening
Look to my heart, not my mind, make me better.
Heaven's reward, not to be earned, this I know.
The Grace of God, His kindness to me,
He constantly doth show.
Monday — Friday, Friday — Monday, a day
Which doth count the most.
Forgetting I do, one's enough, to be lived at all cost.
Weeks, months, years lumped together all
Is enough to make the best of men fall.
As the days go by, I've asked my Lord
Language to use, words to speak
A day, this day, to live
Every flowing from mind to mouth.
Even trying to live and let live, and live, while continuing to live
Only life worth living, yes, in the nature of,
The nature of spiritually speaking.

Mother

My Mother, Our Mother, oh Yes, what a Mother is this Mother.
Patience, kindness, love —
Virtues GOD had in mind when on the 12th day of August in
the year of our Lord 1920
To Lucy and Nathan Thomas Schofield was born at 8:30 A.M.
this Mother.

I have never met, spoken to, shudder to imagine a Lady
A Lady like this Lady, such elegance, such grace,
Oh such ladyness, this Lady.
Many gifts God gave to this family, this group, this clan.
Susan McFarland is one of, if not the most precious,
Beautiful gifts
Given to this family, given to any family.

I ask? I ask GOD? How many days have we?
What would we do if we knew what the future would be?
Change what we are? Change how we see? Change to be free?
When I ask, He answers! Oh yes, loudly in my heart,
He answers!
"No number of days matters, son, love matters.
Love of loved ones matters, like the love of a Mother matters,
Yes, the love of a Mother, our Mother, your Mother."

A Dance with Romance

"Come dance a dance of romance with me,"
Said the bumble to the bee.
"For even I will, up on the hill,"
Said Jack to Jill.

Now, Shan, Shan, where came your name from?
Let me guess, the queen of the prom?
If not, I'd know not said your Lancelot.
So, continue on, the path of one
For our heart you've truly won.

Diana, My New Friend

Diana, a friend, a new one indeed
A friend one has, from even or odd
From the Philippines to Greenwood
Quite a distance to cook, a dinner from
A new friend indeed.

As Sunday ends and Monday begins
It may never be the same
As each day brings new life
And new experiences from the coin game.

A nurse is she, a good one you see
Ever moving forward to a point she should be
From this to that and that to this
Ever softly and lightly on the cheek a kiss.

Now if she's kinda shy
And a little reserved
It's just that she's so sweet
And with honor so preserved.

Jessica

Jessica, Jessica, how sweet will be the dinner
How kind to prepare it, serve it, and share it.
The wait too long, the anticipation too keen
As long as it's soon, then I volunteer to clean.

We all have heroes we admire and look up to.
Lauren's big heart points to you.
Her dancing so great, it's tip-top shape.
God's blessed you so much, so very, very much.

Now let's all see how far life goes
We set our sights on the reddest rose.
Ever mindful and thankful that she's all yours
From day one until Jesus comes.

It's been really nice to meet you.
I hope you think it's nice, too.
And when we dance and dine as well,
We'll both have and who can tell?

P.S. And lots of chocolate.

A Seed

As night follows day
As doth day follow night
A point of life and love doth
A point of heart and of wise arise

From whence did they begin, indeed?
Before fruit, before life, before birth
A seed

A seed, a new growth, from planting
And caring — for one, for one another
Much more than lover to lover

As countenance fair, eyes brighter
Future springs from the heart
His singing bursts from joy within
Pray they never part

As creative insight for lights
That shall lead
Ever stemming, while flowing
Ever forward I plead

Whose sower shall harvest?
This fruit this day?
Modest yet sensitive
And bold ones obey

For once more the sun begins to dawn
Another moment closer to heaven we're drawn
Dreams of spiritual unity
In happiness and holiness

God's blessing, as promised
To Adam and Eve
Ever mindful and wonderful
Since the original seed.

Look Up

There are too many moments in life. I look down,
Around and not yet up, so
Look up.
When I do, what she sees, doing that expected of me,
I miss the ride that's supposed to be. So why not avoid the
pain of looking back, leaving off the rest,
Stemming from the past,
Looking not back, but forward, not down, but up.

When you, or I, or even they, or we look down, we miss so
much not found on ground, but above ground, straight high,
high above straight.
I only see my life's circle, not hers, surely not theirs,
Sad not glad, or even mad.
So much I miss looking down, when choices present
Themselves, as in my choice.

When look back I do, oh how far that seems to be, yet so
close to eternity.
Backwards I feel, one step behind another,
I go until a word I say,
From help above coming from not standing, but kneeling.
Not an easy thing to say or do.

Stop

When I act upon this word I look, yes, look up.
I see whites of clouds, blues of skies,
Enough for tears to drip, ease, then flow from eyes, our eyes.

I now realize what beauty is found, experienced, felt
To look, look up at God's clouds, God's skies
Brings happiness to my head, my heart, my soul, yes, my very
own soul.

Walkin, runnin, joggin, skippin, bladin, and other 'in.
Take a look; take a look, a close look at what ya was missin,
by lookin,
Lookin above at where they all are, and where on a day, past
this day
We, we will be...up...up very high, and yet too high.

Knows, who knows, does anyone really know when we will
get there?
Yes, HE knows...when-how-why- and even where.
Wonderful, as before we reach you to Him, HE reaches down
to us.

Thankful that He knows, so very much, so "muy bueno" (very
good . . . Spanish) much.

Next choice presents itself. I pray I don't look down, or even
around, or back,
But up, yes, look, look up.

Ole Rebel Boy

You know it seems as days have gone by
With the problems facing us we'll surely try
At lending a hand, a helping one indeed
To our family and friends when in time of need.

Such a pleasure to be coupled with the man of the year
But it's hard to stand by and continually hear
That this lawyer's work is never done.
As I sit on the sidelines, waiting's no fun!

All my dreams and prayers of my future I see
Coming slowly but surely to the point they should be,
When "Ole Rebel Boy" moves over, and I take over.
What a day that day will be!

So you see, my friend, as this day's gone by,
The love between us has stood the time.
As you clearly see from our friendship today,
It's continued and grown since my first birthday.

Woman of the Year

To the most lovely and affectionate woman this day,
A humble man and pen would like to say
We give you our thanks for all the times
You've poured out your heart and been so kind.

Too much can't be said without drawing a tear.
Through all our lives she's brought us cheer
And comforted so through trial and tribulation.
Prayer, Church, Choir — A leader in our congregation.

Mothers throughout would be proud of this one,
Hustling and sweating, she's a true tennis bum!
Her quickness erratic, her strength inconsistent.
We've talked to her partner: she's very persistent.

The jokes are fun, and fun's okay.
But to tell the truth, we'll have to say
This Mother's so sweet, the world should hear
We couple them into stardom announcing her
"Woman of the Year."

"Though I speak with the tongues of men and angels and have not love, I am become as a sounding brass and a clanging cymbal."

1 Corinthians 13:1

"The human heart is like a ship on a stormy sea driven about by winds blowing from all Four Corners of Heaven."

Martin Luther

"The heart that loves is always young."
Anonymous (Greek proverb)

"What is life without the radiance of love?"

J. C. F. von Schiller

Divine Intervention

With light so dim as silence hear
I ask my Maker the way
Far ahead the view I pierce
That opened from yesterday

From years and years ago, mistakes abound
Too, too many to count
For then had life of mine ended
Worst chapter, thus saved to last

However, Grace and Mercy truly abound
For forever forgiving, and thanksgiving I'm really glad
That today — a new day —
No longer am I sad

As truth stands tall, for even I feel
Justice no longer I demand
Grace and Mercy — receive I will
As Father in Heaven holds my hand

From Where Did You Come?

Out of nowhere, without notice,
Do tell from where did you come?
Eyes, yes, deep that sparkle, so delightful,
Only moments in thought came ever so cheerful.

One step, one move, the slightest glance
To a place, hidden forever's last chance.

Wonder and phases and share so dear
Nights reading brings
To leave, to leave from there
If thou canst only sit, sit here.

Scarcely the laughter behind the face
As the smile peeks ever so slightly
Turn and walk does she
Ever gleaming so brightly.

Silent and still return from eve
Do now tell from where did you come?
Out of nowhere? Out of here? Or out of there?

"There is no fear in love; but perfect love **casteth** out fear."

1 John 4:18

"Two souls with but a single thought,
Two hearts beat as one."

Marie Lovell

"I was a child and she was a child —
In this Kingdom by the sea.
But we loved with a love that was more than love
I and my Annabel Lee."

Edgar Allan Poe

"Oh, my luve's like a red red rose
That's newly sprung in June:
Oh, my luve's like the melodie
That's sweetly played in June."

Robert Burns

The Butterfly

I am not sure where this piece came from. If I knew I would tell you, but I don't, so I can't. I thought it was so good that I wouldn't let the lack of authorship keep me from sharing it with you. I can only tell you it didn't originate with me, okay?

A man found a cocoon of a butterfly. One day a small opening appeared. The man sat and watched the butterfly for several hours as it struggled to force its body through that little hole. Then it seemed to stop making any progress. It appeared as if it had gotten as far as it could, and it could go no farther. So the man decided to help the butterfly. He took a pair of scissors and snipped off the remaining bit of the cocoon. The butterfly then emerged easily. But it had a swollen body and small shriveled wings. The man continued to watch the butterfly, because he expected that, at any moment, the wings would enlarge and expand to be able to support the body, which would contract in time. Neither happened. In fact, the butterfly spent the rest of its life crawling around with a swollen body and shriveled wings. It never was able to fly. What the man, in his kindness and haste, did not understand was that the restricting cocoon and the struggle required for the butterfly to get through the tiny opening were God's way of forcing fluid from the body of the butterfly into its wings, so that it would be ready for flight once it achieved its freedom from the cocoon.

Sometimes struggles are exactly what we need in our lives.

If God allowed us to go through our lives without any obstacles, it would cripple us. We would not be as strong as what we could have been. We could never fly!

I asked for Strength, and God gave me Difficulties to make me strong.

I asked for Wisdom, and God gave me Problems to solve.

I asked for Prosperity, and God gave me Brain and Brawn to work.

I asked for Courage, and God gave me Danger to overcome.

I asked for Love, and God gave me Troubled People to help.

I asked for Favors, and God gave me Opportunities.

I received nothing that I wanted. I received everything I needed!

May God Bless You.

May God bless you with unspeakable joy, not only in the world to come, but in this world, also. May your path be bright and full of light everywhere you go. May God tell darkness that it must flee at your command. And I pray your feet will never stumble out of God's plan. May the desires of your heart come true. And may you experience Peace in everything you do. May Goodness, Kindness, and Mercy come your way.

Tomorrow's Promise

As we think of all God's blessings of yesterday, miracles and protection, it is not unusual to be astounded by the loving Grace our good "Lord Jesus Christ" has shown us. Continuing to realize what He has done for us, we are honored, as we are thankful for what is taking place now, today, this moment, this very moment. He watches over us, His children, ever so closely. I am reminded by those who live their lives like Pete Dela Riva and Mary Parker, both of Jackson, Mississippi, whose shining examples of enthusiasm and inspiration speak loudly for God's daily gift.

His ultimate blessing of Grace and Love is yet to come. Yes, the gift above all others of mankind is wrapped in the package of "Tomorrow's Promise." Each year, each second, each week, each quarter, each month, each day, you can truly feel it. Is it a time, is it a place? For now, if you are reading this, it remains a promise, a promise of tomorrow, tomorrow's promise.

Heaven

I am thankful that GOD, the only GOD, your GOD and my GOD, our GOD, has saved the best for last, that shall not end but will in fact last, last forever. Hitting my knees, I ask Him, my best friend, for insight to say not the wrong thing but the right, as we talk. In doing so I am reminded, as long as I can remember that whenever I use all my wisdom, understanding, etc. to make an important statement, it seems to come out backward at best. On the other hand, when I depend on the following: "For the Holy Spirit will teach you in that very hour what you ought to say," (Luke 12:12)...or "I will instruct you and teach you in the way which you should go: I will counsel you with my eye upon you," (Psalms 32:8)...or "For it is not you who speak, but it is the Spirit of your Father who speaks in you," (Matt. 10:20) ...or "And when they arrest you and deliver you up, do not be anxious before hand about what you are to say, but say whatever is given you in that hour; for it is not you who speak, but it is the Holy Spirit," (Mark 13:11)...or even, "Now then go, I even I will be with your mouth, and teach you what you are to say," (Exodus 4:12)...whatever I say seems to come out much better, so much better, that I believe more so than I believe my name, that GOD can, will, and does put-words-in-my-mouth, words-in-your-mouth, words-in-our-mouths, now and forever.

Introduction to "The Song of Solomon"

The Song of Songs or The Song of Solomon, authored by Solomon, many think is one of, if not the, most spiritually romantic works. It is the 22nd Book in the New Testament of The Bible, just after Ecclesiastes and before Isaiah. The song is about love, not your run-of-the-mill love, but a love that is on a very high level. When we read it, we further dream of it, we pray a portion one day happens to us. Greens are greener, blues are bluer, and you feel like a kid again, because love as such has encompassed your being like no other feeling. This is not like anything before or anything after. This is it!

Much of the conversation is between the "Beloved" woman and her "Lover," a man. Others join in as well, friends or those close acquaintances. The initial stage is full of kissing, loving, and pursuit. As the distance between the two shortens, both praise and honor the other as one who is flattered and encouraged to come closer.

The dialogue (realizing the point of time in history) from him to her is one of extreme enticement as well as one honoring and recognizing her radiant beauty. It would be quite uncommon to hear today's gentleman woo or court a lady by noticing her hair was like a flock of goats, her teeth like a flock of sheep, her temples like halves of a pomegranate, her neck like a tower, or her breasts like two fans, even if he were referring to her ever lovely and flowing black hair, saintly white teeth, bright rosy face, tremendous being itself, and tender sensuous body.

The love described is what you and I want most of the time, what we aspire to receive and give. The beauty of the words themselves sing as thousands of years have passed since last they were spoken. Speaking of this let them speak for themselves as written, word for word, first verse to last in *The American Standard Holy Bible*.

The Song of Solomon

CHAPTER 1

The Song of Songs, which is Solomon's.
"May he kiss me with the kisses of his mouth!
For your love is better than wine.
Your oils have a pleasing fragrance,
Your name is like purified oil;
Therefore the maidens love you.
Draw me after you and let us run together!
The king has brought me into his chambers."
"We will rejoice in you and be glad;
We will extol your love more than wine.
Rightly do they love you."
I am black but lovely, O daughters of Jerusalem,
Like the tents of Kedar,
Like the curtains of Solomon.
"Do not stare at me because I am swarthy,
For the sun has burned me.
My mother's sons were angry with me;
They made me caretaker of the vineyards,
But I have not taken care of my own vineyard.
"Tell me, O you whom my soul loves,
Where do you make it lie down at noon?
For why should I be like one who veils herself
Beside the flocks of your companions?"

If you yourself do not know,
Most beautiful among women,
Go forth on the trail of the flock,
And pasture your young goats
By the tents of the shepherds.
"To me, my darling, you are like
My mare among the chariots of Pharaoh.
"Your cheeks are lovely with ornaments,
Your neck with strings of beads."
"We will make for you ornaments of gold
With beads of silver."
"While the king was at his table,
My perfume gave forth its fragrance.
"My beloved is to me a pouch of myrrh
Which lies all night between my breasts.
"My beloved is to me a cluster of henna blossoms
In the vineyards of Engedi."
"How beautiful you are, my darling,
How beautiful you are!
Your eyes are like doves."
"How handsome you are, my beloved,
And so pleasant!
Indeed, our couch is luxuriant!
"The beams of our houses are cedars,
Our rafters, cypresses.

CHAPTER   2

"I am the rose of Sharon,
The lily of the valleys."
"Like a lily among the thorns,
So is my darling among the maidens."
"Like an apple tree among the trees of the forest,
So is my beloved among the young men.
In his shade I took great delight and sat down,
And his fruit was sweet to my taste.
"He has brought me to his banquet hall,
And his banner over me is love.
"Sustain me with raisin cakes,
Refresh me with apples,
Because I am lovesick.
"Let his left hand be under my head
And his right hand embrace me."
"I adjure you, O daughters of Jerusalem,
By the gazelles or by the hinds of the field,
That you will not arouse or awaken my love,
Until she pleases."
"Listen! My beloved!
Behold, he is coming,
Climbing on the mountains,
Leaping on the hills!
"My beloved is like a gazelle or a young stag.
Behold, he is standing behind our wall,
He is looking through the windows,
He is peering through the lattice.

"My beloved responded and said to me,
'Arise, my darling, my beautiful one,
And come along.
'For behold, the winter is past,
The rain is over and gone.
'The flowers have already appeared in the land;
The time has arrived for pruning the vines,
And the voice of the turtledove has been heard in our land.
'The fig tree has ripened its figs,
And the vines in blossom have given forth their fragrance.
Arise, my darling, my beautiful one,
And come along!'"
"O, my dove, in the clefts of the rock,
In the secret place of the steep pathway,
Let me see your form,
Let me hear your voice;
For your voice is sweet,
And your form is lovely."
"Catch the foxes for us,
The little foxes that are ruining the vineyards,
While our vineyards are in blossom."
"My beloved is mine, and I am his;
He pastures his flock among the lilies.
"Until the cool of the day when the shadows flee away,
Turn, my beloved, and be like a gazelle
Or a young stag on the mountains of Bether."

CHAPTER 3

"On my bed night after night I sought him
Whom my soul loves;
I sought him but did not find him.
'I must arise now and go about the city;
In the streets and in the squares
I must seek him whom my soul loves.'"
I sought him but did not find him.
"The watchmen who make the rounds in the city found me,
And I said, 'Have you seen him whom my soul loves?'"
"Scarcely had I left them
When I found him whom my soul loves;
I held on to him and would not let him go,
Until I had brought him to my mother's house,
And into the room of her who conceived me."
"I adjure you, O daughters of Jerusalem,
By the gazelles or by the hinds of the field,
That you will not arouse or awaken my love,
Until she pleases."
"What is this coming up from the wilderness
Like columns of smoke,
Perfumed with myrrh and frankincense,
With all scented powders of the merchant?
"Behold, it is the traveling couch of Solomon;
Sixty mighty men around it,
Of the mighty men of Israel.
"All of them are wielders of the sword,
Expert in war;

Each man has his sword at his side,
Guarding against the terrors of the night.
"King Solomon has made for himself a sedan chair
From the timber of Lebanon.
"He made its posts of silver,
Its back of gold
And its seat of purple fabric,
With its interior lovingly fitted out
By the daughters of Jerusalem.
"Go forth, O daughters of Zion,
And gaze on King Solomon with the crown
With which his mother has crowned him
On the day of his wedding,
And on the day of his gladness of heart."

CHAPTER 4

"How beautiful you are, my darling,
How beautiful you are!
Your eyes are like doves behind your veil;
Your hair is like a flock of goats
That have descended from Mount Gilead.
"Your teeth are like a flock of newly shorn ewes
Which have come up from their washing,
All of which bear twins,
And not one among them has lost her young.
"Your lips are like a scarlet thread,
And your mouth is lovely.
Your temples are like a slice of pomegranate

Behind your veil.
"Your neck is like the tower of David
Built with rows of stones,
On which are hung a thousand shields,
All the round shields of the mighty men.
"Your two breasts are like two fawns,
Twins of a gazelle,
Which feed among the lilies.
"Until the cool of the day
When the shadows flee away,
I will go my way to the mountain of myrrh
And to the hill of frankincense.
"You are altogether beautiful, my darling,
And there is no blemish in you.
"Come with me from Lebanon, my bride,
May you come with me from Lebanon.
Journey down from the summit of Amana,
From the summit of Senir and Hermon,
From the dens of lions,
From the mountains of leopards.
"You have made my heart beat faster, my sister, my bride;
You have my heart beat faster with a single
glance of your eyes,
With a single strand of your necklace.
"How beautiful is your love, my sister, my bride!
How much better is your love than wine,
And the fragrance of your oils
Than all kinds of spices!
"Your lips, my bride, drip honey;

Honey and milk are under your tongue,
And the fragrance of your garments is like the
fragrance of Lebanon.
"A garden locked is my sister, my bride,
A rock garden locked, a spring sealed up.
"Your shoots are an orchard of pomegranates
With choice fruits, henna with nard plants,
Nard and saffron, calamus and cinnamon,
With all the trees of frankincense,
Myrrh and aloes, along with all the finest spices.
"You are a garden spring,
A well of fresh water,
And streams flowing from Lebanon."
"Awake, O north wind,
And come, wind of the south;
Make my garden breathe out fragrance,
Let its spices be wafted abroad.
May my beloved come into his garden
And eat its choice fruits!"

CHAPTER 5

"I have come into my garden, my sister, my bride.
I have gathered my myrrh along with my balsam.
I have eaten my honeycomb and my honey;
I have drunk my wine and my milk.
Eat, friends;
Drink and imbibe deeply, O lovers."
"I was asleep, but my heart was awake.

A voice! My beloved was knocking:
  'Open to me, my sister, my darling,
    My dove, my perfect one!
  For my head is drenched with dew,
  My locks with the damp of the night.'
    "I have taken off my dress,
      How can I put it on again?
    I have washed my feet,
      How can I dirty them again?
"My beloved extended his hand through the opening,
  And my feelings were aroused for him.
    "I arose to open to my beloved;
  And my hands dripped with myrrh,
  And my fingers with liquid myrrh,
    On the handles of the bolt.
    "I opened to my beloved,
But my beloved had turned away and had gone!
  My heart went out to him as he spoke.
I searched for him, but I did not find him;
  I called him, but he did not answer me.
"The watchmen who make the rounds in the city found me,
  They struck me and wounded me.
The guardsmen of the walls took away my shawl from me.
    "I adjure you, O daughters of Jerusalem,
      If you find my beloved,
      As to what you will tell him:
      For I am lovesick."
    "What kind of beloved is your beloved,
    O most beautiful among women?

What kind of beloved is your beloved,
That thus you adjure us?"
"My beloved is dazzling and ruddy,
Outstanding among ten thousand.
"His head is like gold, pure gold;
His locks are like clusters of dates,
And black as a raven.
"His eyes are like doves,
Beside streams of water,
Bathed in milk,
And reposed in their setting.
"His cheeks are like a bed of balsam,
Banks of sweet-scented herbs;
His lips are lilies,
Dripping with liquid myrrh.
"His hands are rods of gold
Set with beryl;
His abdomen is carved ivory
Inlaid with sapphires.
"His legs are pillars of alabaster
Set on pedestals of pure gold;
His appearance is like Lebanon,
Choice as the cedars.
"His mouth is full of sweetness.
And he is wholly desirable.
This is my beloved and this is my friend,
O daughters of Jerusalem."

CHAPTER 6

"Where has your beloved gone,
O most beautiful of women?
Where has your beloved turned,
That we may seek him with you?"
"My beloved has gone down to his garden,
To the beds of balsam,
To pasture his flock in the gardens
And gather lilies.
"I am my beloved's and my beloved is mine,
He who pastures his flock among the lilies."
"You are as beautiful as Tirzah, my darling,
As lovely as Jerusalem,
As awesome as an army with banners.
"Turn your eyes away from me,
For they have confused me;
Your hair is like a flock of goats
That have descended from Gilead.
"Your teeth are like a flock of ewes
Which have come up from their washing,
All of which bear twins,
And not one among them has lost her young.
"Your temples are like a slice of pomegranate
Behind your veil.
"There are sixty queens and eighty concubines,
And maidens without number;
But my dove, my perfect one, is unique:
She is her mother's only daughter;

She is the pure child of the one who bore her.
The maidens saw her and called her blessed,
The queens and the concubines also, and they praised her,
saying,
'Who is this that grows like the dawn,
As beautiful as the full moon,
As pure as the sun,
As awesome as an army with banners?'
"I went down to the orchard of nut trees
To see the blossoms of the valley,
To see whether the vine had budded
Or the pomegranates had bloomed.
"Before I was aware, my soul set me
Over the chariots of my noble people."
"Come back, come back, O Shulammite;
Come back, come back, that we may gaze at you!"
"Why should you gaze at the Shulammite,
As at the dance of the two companies?"

CHAPTER 7

"How beautiful are your feet in sandals,
O prince's daughter!
The curves of your hips are like jewels,
The work of the hands of an artist.
"Your navel is like a round goblet
Which never lacks mixed wine;
Your belly is like a heap of wheat
Fenced about with lilies.

"Your two breasts are like two fawns,
Twins of a gazelle.
"Your neck is like a tower of ivory,
Your eyes like the pools in Heshbon
By the gate of Bath-rabbim;
Your nose is like the tower of Lebanon,
Which faces toward Damascus.
"Your head crowns you like Carmel,
And the flowing locks of your head are like purple threads;
The king is captivated by your tresses.
"How beautiful and how delightful you are,
My love, with all your charms!
"Your stature is like a palm tree,
And your breasts are like its clusters.
"I said, 'I will climb the palm tree,
I will take hold of its fruit stalks.'
Oh, may your breasts be like clusters of the vine,
And the fragrance of your breath like apples,
And your mouth like the best wine!"
"It goes down smoothly for my beloved,
Flowing gently through the lips of those who fall asleep.
"I am my beloved's,
And his desire is for me.
"Come, my beloved, let us go out into the country,
Let us spend the night in the villages.
"Let us rise early and go to the vineyards;
Let us see whether the vine has budded
And its blossoms have opened,
And whether the pomegranates have bloomed.

There I will give you my love.
"The mandrakes have given forth fragrance;
And over our doors are all choice fruits,
Both new and old,
Which I have saved up for you, my beloved.

CHAPTER 8

.

"Oh that you were like a brother to me
Who nursed at my mother's breasts.
If I found you outdoors, I would kiss you;
No one would despise me, either.
"I would lead you and bring you
Into the house of my mother, who used to instruct me;
I would give you spiced wine to drink from the
juice of my pomegranates.
"Let his left hand be under my head, and his right hand
embrace me."
"I want you to swear, O daughters of Jerusalem,
Do not arouse or awaken my love,
Until she pleases."
"Who is this coming up from the wilderness,
Leaning on her beloved?"
"Beneath the apple tree I awakened you;
There your mother was in labor with you,
There she was in labor and gave you birth.
"Put me like a seal over your heart,
Like a seal on your arm.
For love is as strong as death,

Jealousy is as severe as Sheol;
Its flashes are flashes of fire,
The very flame of the Lord.
"Many waters cannot quench love,
Nor will rivers overflow it;
If a man were to give all the riches of his house for love,
It would be utterly despised."
"We have a little sister,
And she has no breasts;
What shall we do for our sister
On the day she is spoken for?
"If she is a wall,
We shall build on her a battlement of silver;
But if she is a door,
We shall barricade her with planks of cedar."
"I was a wall, and my breasts were like towers;
Then I became in his eyes as one who finds peace.
"Solomon had a vineyard at Baal-hamon;
He entrusted the vineyard to caretakers;
Each one was to bring a thousand shekels of silver for its fruit.
"My very own vineyard is at my disposal;
The thousand shekels are for you, Solomon,
And two hundred are for those who take care of its fruit."
"O you who sit in the gardens,
My companions are listening for your voice —
Let me hear it!"
"Hurry, my beloved,
And be like a gazelle or a young stag
On the mountains of spices."

I am so amazed each time I re-read Solomon's Songs and especially each time I re-type them. I am not a rather slow typist. I am in fact a slow typist, who is accompanied by the advantage of allowing words as such to gradually soak in, savoring their beauty. My amazement of the "songs" stems from thousands of hundreds and hundreds of thousands of stories, poems, and songs that have been written throughout the ages about romance, love, and the pursuit thereof that do not even touch the affection, gentleness, excitement, anticipation, intimacy, and intensity that the above has, not even in the same ballpark are many . . . best-sellers.

"A fool there was and he made his prayer even as you and I.
To a rag and a bone and a hank of hair we called her the
woman who didn't care.
But the fool called her his lady fair, even as you and I."

Rudard Kipling

"Love suffereth long and is kind; love envieth not;
love vaunteth not itself; is not puffed up."

1 Corinthians 13:4

"One word frees us of all the weight and pain of all life.
That word is love."

Sophocles

Daddy or Un-Daddy-Like ?

John, as in *Webster's,* tells us both what words mean, and when one needs a source to cite, what better one to use than his? When I look up "spiritual," he says that deals with the "soul," and a couple pages prior, he says soul means a person with lots of feelings.

On December 5, 1988, at 7:00 A.M., my spiritual soul was fine until my son and hero, Robert, went to the bus stop for junior high school with my daughter and hero, Anna. Robert had missed the day before, sick, and I stayed home from my law office in spite of the fact the most important case thus far in my career was in the final stages of conclusion.

I needed to be at my office preparing for this most important conference, scheduled for 10:00 that morning. I told Robert specifically not to get wet even though it was raining. "Stay dry. I mean it."

To be on the safe side, I drove by the bus stop, where to my extreme displeasure, I found him laughing, playing in the rain with his friends. I drove up and really let him know how unhappy I was with his actions, raising my voice in disapproval and discipline. He stepped over to me with a little-hurt-look in his eyes, with tears running down his cheeks; told me I was embarrassing him. Without responding to him, I just said we would finish this when I got home. Before I got out of the parking lot, I felt an empty feeling in my gut. On the way to my office, attempts to forget by listening to the radio and even talking tapes failed. I could not concentrate, and the closer I got to 10:00, the more distant and distraught I became. I could stand it no longer. Bobby Jo, my only co-worker at the time, who is also basically my twin, said, "Go, go. Missing this meeting can do no worse to you than you are doing to yourself. I'll figure something out." I had to go and find my son and tell him how sorry I was and how I had been so un-daddy-like. As I type and revisit these feelings, the nausea and tears I felt returns, since only 13 years have passed since that day.

I went to his school, and the principal sent him to meet me in the cafeteria, where we were by ourselves. As one could imagine, he wanted to know if he was in trouble, to which I responded, "No son, it is not you who is in trouble. I am so sorry that I was ugly and hurt your feelings this morning. I was very wrong. No lawyers matter, no contract matters, no judge matters, and no job matters. The only thing that matters now is you."

Like the true Champion he was then and is today, he put his little arms around my neck and told me it was okay and that he and Anna were real glad I was their Daddy. You know, he was right. It turned out okay and still is now. Before then I felt so bad and sad, and afterwards I felt so glad and happy. I would not trade that moment then or now for all the gold in all the hills. God so freely gives us more blessings than we can ever count. Isn't that wonderful?

You know, life sure is mighty funny sometimes, since shortly after that God caused to find its way into my hands, a great book written by one of, if not, the most successful inspiring motivators in modern time, Dale Carnegie. In his book, *How to*

Win Friends and Influence People, he concludes the first chapter by the following:

> Often parents are tempted to criticize their children. You would expect me to say don't, but I will not. I am merely going to say, "Before you criticize them read one of the classics of American journalism, "Father Forgets."

It originally appeared in the *People's Homes Journal*. We are reprinting it here with the author's permission, as condensed in *Reader's Digest*.

"Father Forgets," by W. Livingston Larned, is one of those little pieces which, dashed off in a moment of sincere feeling, strikes an echoing chord in so many readers as to become a perennial reprint favorite. Since its first appearance, "Father Forgets" has been reproduced in hundreds of magazines and house organs and in newspapers throughout the country. It has also been reprinted almost as extensively in many foreign languages. He has given permission to thousands who wished to read it from school, church, and lecture platforms. It has been on the air on countless occasions and programs. Oddly enough, college periodicals have used it and high school magazines. Sometimes a little piece seems mysteriously to 'click.' This one certainly did.

Father Forgets

W. Livingston Larned

Listen, son: I am saying this as you lie asleep, one little paw crumpled under your cheek and the blonde curls stickily wet on your damp forehead. I have stolen into your room alone. Just a few minutes ago, as I sat reading my paper, a stifling wave of remorse swept over me. Guiltily I came to your bedside.

These are the things I was thinking, son; I had been too cross to you. I scolded you as you were dressing for school because you gave your face merely a dab with a towel. I took you to task for not cleaning your shoes. I called out angrily when you threw some of your things on the floor.

At breakfast I found fault, too. You spilled things, too. You gulped down your food. You put your elbows on the table. You spread your butter too thick on your bread. And as you started off to play and made for the train you turned and waved a hand and called, "Goodbye Daddy!" and I frowned and said in reply, "Hold your shoulders back!" Then it began again all over again in the late afternoon. As I came up the road, I spied you down on your knees, playing marbles. There were holes in your stockings. I humiliated you before your boyfriends by marching you ahead of me to the house. Stockings were expensive — and if you had to buy them you would be more careful! Imagine that son, from a father!

Do you remember, later when I was reading in the library,

you came in timidly, with a sort of hurt look in your eye? When I glanced over my paper, impatient at the interruption, you hesitated at the door, "What is it you want?" I snapped.

You said nothing, but ran across with one tempestuous plunge, and threw your arms around my neck and kissed me, and your small arms tightened with affection that God had sent blooming into your heart and which even neglect could not wither. And then you were gone, pattering up the stairs.

Well, son, it was shortly after that my paper slipped from my hands and a terrible sinking fear came over me. What has habit been doing to me? The habit of finding fault, of reprimanding this was my reward to you for being a boy. It was not that I did not love you: it was that I expected too much of youth. I was measuring you by the yardstick of my own years.

And there was so much that was good and fine and true in your character. The little heart of yours was as big as the dawn itself over the wide hills. This was shown by your spontaneous impulse to rush in and kiss me goodnight. Nothing else matters tonight, son. I have come to your bedside in the darkness, and I have knelt here ashamed!

It is a feeble atonement; I know you would not understand these things if I told them to you during your waking hours. But tomorrow I will be a real daddy! I will chum with you, and suffer when you suffer, and will laugh when you laugh, cry when you cry. I will bite my tongue when impatient words come. I will keep saying as it were a ritual: "He is nothing but a boy — a little boy!"

I'm afraid I have visualized you as a man. Yet as I see you now, son, crumpled and weary in your cot, I see that you are still a baby. Yesterday you were in your mother's arms, your head on her shoulder. I have asked too much, too much.

Instead of condemning people, let's try to understand them. Let's try to figure out why they do what they do. That's a lot more profitable and intriguing than criticism; and it breeds sympathy, tolerance, and kindness. "To know all is to forgive all."

As Dr. Johnson said, "God Himself, sir, does not propose to judge a man until the end of his days."

Why should you and I?

Loving and Losing, or What Barnes & Noble Means to Me in a Personal Sense

I've always enjoyed going to our country's main book store and current popular hangout, Barnes & Noble. It was only recently that this establishment of reading, relaxing, drinking of coffee, meeting of friends, as well as the making of new ones had such a profound effect on my life in the arena of loving and losing.

You know, a very healthy trend in our country is away from going to bars all over town, getting drunk, and meeting people, primarily of the opposite sex. Many feel this speaks highly of the direction we are heading. It sure does make the highways safer to go from this point to that. This still leaves for many the desire to frequent places others frequent, especially those of the opposite sex, which is one of the reasons for the increased popularity of book stores, especially Barnes & Noble, which also serves Starbucks coffee and some of the finest chocolate you have ever put in your mouth (my favorite is 'chocolate decadence'... a real sweet treat), served in a very friendly manner by Carrie or Courtney, from behind the desert counter in Shreveport, Louisiana.

On January 14th, 1999, at 7:30 P.M., I was sitting on County Line Road, in Jackson, Mississippi, in one of the over 500 Barnes & Nobles, eating some real fine, high-grade chocolate and sipping on a tall, hot cup of coffee, one of the sweetest drinks in town. Since I was sitting at a quaint table in the dessert area, I couldn't help but notice the serving area where a lady was ordering some of what appeared to be the same hot coffee and sweet chocolate. The more I noticed her, the less I paid attention to anything or anyone else, until I could wait no longer and felt it necessary to try and introduce myself. I would bet $100, American money, against a donut that on more than one occasion you have seen someone and had given anything to meet them, maybe not really "anything," but it just seemed that way at the time.

How do things happen — as chance would have it, or as life unfolds, or as God causes to occur? When it comes to relationships I am not nearly as sure of the differences as I am with business ideas or other events. I spoke to her, met her, liked her, dated her and fell in love with her. To no one's surprise, Barnes & Noble was our favorite place to meet, hang out, hold hands, stare in each other's eyes. We would get travel and adventure books with lots of color pictures, as we dreamed and planned our lives together. The blues were bluer and the greens were greener, and when we woke in the morning most days seemed like a holiday, you know? I bet you do.

It's funny: from Birmingham, Alabama, to Cheyenne, Wyoming, and from The World's Largest Bookstore on Fifth Avenue in New York to Sunset Place in Miami, and other sites where Barnes & Noble makes its home would be a good place to visit, knowing that there would at least be one thing familiar to us. As God continued to say good morning by the rising of the sun and goodnight by its setting, we grew to know and love each other more each day.

At 8:35 P.M., Friday June 12th, I had prearranged for Kevin Myers, an employee, personal friend, and cool guy as well, to be on County Line Road in the Barnes & Noble coffee shop, armed with fully loaded camera aimed at the small quaint table where we first sat. We entered together, ordered our usual dessert, as if we were going to a movie all dressed up, then sat at "our table." I got on my knee, and with all the happiness and dreams of the future, I asked her to do me the ultimate honor and take my hand in marriage. I remember it now as if only moments ago. I was in that Barnes & Noble store where it had seemed like my backyard to my home, and that this life could not get any better. I felt I was on cloud nine's cloud nine. She wholeheartedly said yes, and Kevin began the photo family album.

As time continued to pass, we came to believe that God had a soul mate of love for each of us, but it just was not each other. That was quite the painful experience for both of us. My fiancée left town. I didn't.

When I was growing up I had some horses I really liked riding, and occasionally I would get bucked off. Many who knew more than I did said to go ahead and immediately get back on, and I would. I can tell you it was a lot easier getting back on those horses than it was going back between those two swinging doors at Barnes & Noble into what had become for me the most fun, frequented place, except the Church. As Tennyson said, "It is better to have loved and lost than never to have loved at all." And I had to ask myself what have I, in fact, lost? The answer continued to show gains instead of losses. After about a week, I felt kind of embarrassed, and uncomfortable, but went back to my writing and reading groups. It took a while but now the coffee is more delicious and the chocolate sweeter than it has ever been, and occasionally I can't help but keep my eye on that one particular table in the dessert area.

"I'm Just Not That Smart"

So, so many times in my life things have happened to me, around me, and on behalf of me that were astounding, bordering on "hard-to-believe." I do believe. I believe my ears have not deceived me when those I like and even those I don't say to me "Wow, that sure is smart," "Gee, that was brilliant," "Man, that was very wise." At moments like these, many things I know not, but one I know; "I'm just not that smart."

It is not a personal insult for me to say about myself that left to my own devices I would be an accident looking for a place to happen. I do not mind realizing that of myself I am nothing. It is actually a relief knowing that if I am all I have, all I have is me, and that is not enough — by no means. What I need, what I am going to have no matter what is a wonderful, miraculous Heavenly Father who loves me enough to forgive me when I cannot love or forgive myself. He has shown me through you and others that "life is to be lived large," to quote a great friend of mine, J. J. Sanchez.

My son Robert said of J. J. the following, "Dad, you have got to meet my new friend J. J. He is the greatest guy you will ever know. If wars were decided by men, and half the men had a heart half the size of J. J.'s...there would be NO MORE WARS." In spite of his Cerebral Palsy he lives life large. After we met, the following events led him to being the man of the hour for two years (1997 and 1998) as my company, HealthOne, sponsored a

Pro-Am celebrity LPGA golf tournament, the only LPGA event in Mississippi until the U.S. Open in 1999. It was named the "J. J. Sanchez-HealthOne Celebrity Classic featuring stars of the LPGA and benefiting Cerebral Palsy." The event was great and helped many lives especially many children with this condition in Mississippi. The idea and vision appeared to originate with me, and I can promise you "I'm just not that smart".

In 1987 I moved to Nashville, Tennessee and as an associate, prior to that time with limited experience, I served as Chief Counsel to the law firm which represented the business office of Vanderbilt Hospital, one of the finest hospitals in the country, one of the greatest legal-medical jobs anywhere. After a short time in the field, it became apparent to me that a flaw existed in the legal-medical circle. In short when a patient enters a hospital as the result of an accident, they sign the admission form that basically states "I promise to pay." That's it. The patient is then discharged, often with a large bill, and hires an attorney. Then they together make demands on the liability insurance carrier for the proceeds of the policy to take care of the medical bill, pain and suffering, etc. They get the money earmarked for the hospital and keep it. The more this happened on cases of my clients, the hospitals, the more offended I became.

I researched, fought, screamed, cried, looked to kick a dog and found none (much to the pleasure of the canine population). I meditated and prayed for a solution. In 1994, after seven years of frustration while struggling with this issue, I became obsessed and completely consumed with the search for an answer. It came. I had it in my mind and my heart. God blessed me with a vision that has gradually, since that time, begun to change our industry in this arena. After the idea was presented, my Dad, my hero, and the smartest and most respected 'Southern Gentleman' I have ever known, informed me that if this involved half the magnitude it appeared to have, that it would be great for healthcare, and maybe if it was really successful, maybe at a banquet I would possibly receive some sort of semi-attractive plaque or maybe a mention in a monthly magazine, but it would not go far in satisfying the indebtedness created by the pursuit. Therefore, on August 28, 1995, I applied to the Office of Copyright in Washington D.C. to protect the language used in establishing this unique and superior position for the hospital, resulting in granting approval registration (#TXu 700 360). On the same day I also applied to the same government agency covering the procedures in which the language is used, which was likewise accepted and granted under registration # TXu 673 331. After that I got a lot of "ooos and aahs" and "gee-whizzes" and had additional new friends, who until then I didn't even know existed.

The circle of my newly acquired friends increased when in January of 1997 Michael Tanner, Director of the Health and Welfare Division of the Cato Institute (what many believe to be the #1 think-tank in the world) in Washington, completed a study on me and my company. He reported all positive findings including "There are often small changes that can have a significant impact on healthcare costs. Changing the way hospitals and courts treat third-party liability cases is one of these small changes that can have big results." The article appeared in the national publication *Washington Times,* "Insight on the News," August 4, 1997. Similar articles appeared individually in about 25 states.

The reason I share a small portion of information about my company's history with you is to emphasize the grace and love Jesus Christ has shown me, my family, and our friends. I think you would agree we don't go to Heaven by being "rich and/or famous," and the chance is good that's good news for both of us.

May I ask whether you have ever had something happen to you that seemed so great it was hard to believe that something so wonderful not only could, but did happen to you? Have you lately been in a real tight situation that didn't seem to have any route out, but there was? When was the last time you told God if just one more time He would help you, and then He did? How do these events take place? Why do such things happen over and over and over again? How about adding the element of us not doing anything to earn such kindness, forgiveness and second, third, and umpteen (I wonder how many outside the south are familiar with this word) chances? I know I am reminded of my wonderful Mother's description of God's grace and tender love, unequalled. GOD, GOD, many praises to the Maker and Creator.

I sometimes believe He feels so sorry for me that He helps me. Other times I wonder if it is my backwardness as well as my hardheadeness. I dream at times HE does it because my Father's Father's Father begged for his son's son's son compassion that would extend to you and me. You know all these may be true, along with thousands and thousands of other reasons. My favorite is that He loved us more than any Father in the truest sense could, and gave us the gift of Himself, His Son, and further that when all our time is done the life we sometimes struggle with has truly been won, as the sweet breath of Heaven blows upon us, not by our efforts, but by His. Most of the time the realization is clear that more of life I do not understand; however, I am absolutely sure that the God I worship, respect, and admire has done more for me than I could ask for, or ever expect, or knew existed. For that I am really grateful, thankful, and happy.

When this my first book began to really come together, I tried to spend a lot of time on my knees thanking our Heavenly Father for the chance to spread-a-little-sunshine, and I asked for the direction to not say the wrong thing, but the right, and to remember that I am to be counted as one of many who believe the following to be one of, if not the most wonderful, inspiring, true, meaningful, beautiful words ever spoken or written: " I can do all things through Jesus Christ who strengthens me." (Philippians 4:13).

Dr. Norman Vincent Peale, one of my favorite authors, who's been in Heaven since 1991, wrote some tremendous books that have had some profound effects upon many, including myself. God used him a lot for a long time, and his book, *The Power of Positive Thinking,* is in my opinion the greatest book ever written except the Bible. Dr. Peale told millions and millions through his many books and magazine *Guideposts* that this verse was best, the best, the very best, above all the rest.

Ever since before I could remember I felt really, really bad when I did something that was not nice and felt very good all over when I did something that was; not necessarily big things. On a couple occasions in the Bible, one is referred to as seeking after God's own heart. I love my son Robert and my daughter Anna more than I can ever express and really understand. I really love my Mommy and Daddy a lot, too, and sisters Bobby Jo, and her wonderful daughter Melissa, and Anna Hart, and Hart and Mark, Anna Hart's children, as I continue to love our sister Suzanne so much. More than all these put together, as well as myself, I love God and seek after His own heart. I don't really have to understand that. I just have to know that. This is the reason I have written this book and in the manner in which I have written it. Thank you for taking your precious and valuable time to read it.

May God bless you, your family, and friends
Now and forever...

— Burns

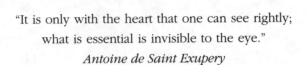

"It is only with the heart that one can see rightly;
what is essential is invisible to the eye."
Antoine de Saint Exupery

"He that loveth not his brother whom he hath seen,
how can he love God whom he hath not seen?"

1 John 4:20

About the Author

Burns Harrison McFarland is a Mississippi attorney, recognized by *The Cato Institute* for his contribution in the legal-medical field of third-party liability. While serving as Chief Counsel of the law firm which represented the business office of Vanderbilt University Medical Center in Nashville, Tennessee, he developed a series of copyrighted procedures and documents concerning patient admission. He was also recognized as one of the country's top healthcare editors in 1997, while editor of Mississippi's Healthcare Financial Management Association publication. He is owner of "Burns & James Original Jezebel Sauce," a company that manufactures and distributes garnish dressing throughout the south. Additionally he owns "Angel on My Shoulder," a retail angel store based in Jackson, Mississippi.

McFarland, during his college days, helped mold the formation of soccer in Mississippi, while serving as one of its earliest presidents. He also holds all University of Mississippi records and numerous Southeastern Conference records as goal-keeper. He lives with his family in Jackson, Mississippi, and Shreveport, Louisiana.

If you would like to buy additional
copies of this book, please contact:

R & A Inspirational Publishing Company
385 Highland Colony Parkway, Suite 100
Ridgland, MS 39157
(601) 206-5534

www.inspirationalpublishing.com